Negotiating Techniques

How to work toward a constructive agreement

Robert F. Guder
Editor

Published by The Economics Press, Inc.
12 Daniel Road, Fairfield, N.J. 07006

Contents

Part III: Strategy and Tactics

Part IV: Team Negotiations

Introduction

This isn't a book for people whose primary job is formal negotiating—such as labor relations people or lawyers. It's written for managers who may not think of themselves as negotiators, but who, in reality, are negotiating every day—not necessarily in formal negotiating sessions, but in their contacts with others in and out of their organization. It will look at basic principles and practices that they can use in their daily activities—on or off the job.

Basically, there are two kinds of negotiations. The first is adversary negotiations, where one side wins and the other side loses. The other is collaborative "win-win" negotiations, where both sides concentrate on solving a problem in a way that is acceptable to everyone. We'll look at both kinds of negotiating and suggest ways in which you can change adversary negotiations into more profitable collaborative ones, where everyone wins.

Please note that in this book we use the word "opponent" to indicate the person you are negotiating with. That's just because it's the most convenient way of referring to "the person on the other side"—but it does not indicate "enemy". In the most productive negotiations, your "opponent" becomes your partner in searching for an agreement that is to the best interest of both parties.

Much of the material in this book is based on *"Common Sense Negotiations"*, a bulletin published biweekly by The Economics Press, Inc., and written by Dr. Ross R. Reck, C.P.M., and Dr. Brian Long, C.P.M.

Part I.

Negotiating Principles

1.

Every manager negotiates

When we think of negotiating, we tend to think of high-powered confrontations between unions and management or between companies involved in setting the terms of corporate mergers or acquisitions. On a different level, we may think of negotiating as the job of sales departments, purchasing departments, or even legal departments, which are involved in making deals and agreements with outsiders as part of their everyday work. We often don't realize that, as managers, negotiating is an important part of our own jobs as well.

Every manager is a negotiator. You probably don't think of yourself that way, and it probably isn't in your job description. But a good deal of your time is spent negotiating with other people in your organization. Negotiation is basically *persuasion*—and you resort to it whenever you don't have the power—or the inclination—to force others to do what you want.

You can order the people who report to you to do

something, but isn't it more effective to persuade them that the change you want will really benefit them as well as the company? And haven't you ever persuaded your own boss to try something new, or negotiated a salary increase—your own or a subordinate's—with higher management?

On a day-to-day basis, contact with other managers is a major part of your job. Studies have shown that as much as half of the average manager's time is spent trying to reach agreement with other managers on matters that affect them all.

When managers are dealing with each other, they're dealing with people who have different bosses, different priorities, different objectives. Obviously, with this kind of relationship, disagreements are bound to develop. And since neither person has authority over the other, differences must be settled by persuasion and negotiation.

This doesn't mean that there are structured negotiating sessions; it's usually much less formal than that. But to do their jobs well, managers have to know how to negotiate satisfactory solutions to their problems and, at the same time, preserve good relationships for the future.

The fact is, all of us do a bit of negotiating every time we conduct business with another person. In our personal lives as well, we negotiate when we are buying or selling a car or a house, or anything else that doesn't have a fixed price. We negotiate with plumbers, carpenters, and other craftsmen when we need a home repair or improvement, or when we want someone to clean out our attic or garage.

We negotiate with travel agents when we are arranging a trip or a vacation. We negotiate with our wives, our husbands, our children, our neighbors. In short, we all are involved in some kind of negotiation almost every day, and our lives will be smoother if we know how to reconcile differences and make a better deal.

2.

Negotiating styles

Many people approach a negotiation as though it were a battle. They marshal their facts, statistics, and arguments, then go forth determined to get as much as they can and give as little as they must during the negotiation. They consider the other party an adversary, and they strive to get what they want at the expense of the other side.

This is win-lose negotiating; one side wins and the other side loses. People who practice it can be identified by their tactics during the negotiation. To begin with, they start out with exorbitantly high demands or ridiculously low offers. They resist making concessions, and when they do, the concession is only a minimal change in their position. They consider any concessions you make as a sign of weakness, and press harder for more. They usually claim to have limited authority, so that any concessions they do make are subject to approval by their superiors. And they may resort to such emotional tactics as shouting, threatening, or walking out in attempt to bully you into accepting their terms.

There are times when you will find yourself in a win-lose negotiation of this kind, so you should know how to deal with it. This book describes many of the tactics used in such adversarial negotiations so you'll know how to defend yourself against them. But there is another style of negotiating that in most cases is far more productive for both sides.

Win-win negotiating

Particularly when you have a continuing relationship with a negotiating opponent, maintaining goodwill is important. Both parties should feel reasonably well satisfied with the result of the negotiation. An opponent who feels taken advantage of may not carry out the agreement with any enthusiasm and may harbor a determination to "get even" in the future.

That's why in most cases the win-win style of negotiating is more effective. In this style, the emphasis is not on defeating an opponent, but rather on solving a problem in a way that is acceptable to both sides.

Collaborative win-win negotiating is possible because people are different. They have different needs, and the needs of the parties to a negotiation often are not really in opposition. The satisfaction of one person's needs does not have to be at the expense of the other person. If both parties try to solve the problem rather than to defeat each other, both can benefit.

The win-win style of negotiating is particularly appropriate when you're dealing with other managers in your organization. You're going to have a continuing relationship with them, and you're going to need their cooperation in the future. You certainly don't want to win an advantage for yourself or your department at the expense of making enemies who will make your life difficult in the months and years ahead.

Negotiations with others in your organization are ideally suited to the collaborative, win-win style of negotiating. You and the person you're dealing with have individual needs and goals, but you both have the good of the organization as the ultimate consideration. Your object is not to do battle with each other, but to find a solution from which both of you will benefit. You can do this by focusing on defeating the problem, rather than defeating each other.

Building trust

The key to creating a climate in which win-win negotiating will be successful lies in your own attitude. You can't have a collaborative negotiation in an atmosphere of mistrust and suspicion; there must first be a climate of mutual trust.

How can you develop trust? It's not always easy, but it can usually be done. In people with whom you have a continuing relationship, you begin before there's any need for negotiating. You deal with them honestly and straightforwardly. You always keep your word. And just as important, you show that you trust *them*.

If you place your trust in others, they will almost always live up to your expectations. That's the way people are. If you approach them with suspicion, they will pull back and become wary themselves. But if your words and actions show that you are confident that they are honest and trustworthy, they'll usually go out of their way to justify your faith in them.

At the beginning of a negotiation, you can set the tone by being friendly, unthreatening, and sincere. Instead of saying, "This is what I want," begin in a relaxed and open manner: "Look, here's the problem we have. I know you agree that we won't gain anything by trying to beat each other's brains out. What we both want is to find a fair and equitable solution that we can both live with. Right?"

Throughout the negotiation, keep the focus on the problem. When positions are getting rigid and there's a danger of reaching an impasse, back off and look for a different solution. "We don't seem to be getting much closer together on this point. Maybe we can approach it differently and see whether we can solve it in another way." Most deadlocks seem to concern money, but there are usually other elements that can be adjusted to make an agreement possible. Will a longer lead time help? Can payments be spread out over a longer period of time? Can the specifications be changed? (We'll discuss this approach more fully in the chapter on "Changing the Package".)

The point is that there are almost always a number of variables in any negotiation. If you are concentrating on solving the problem rather than on defeating your opponent, the variables can often be repackaged in a way that will meet the needs of both parties.

Everybody wins

There are times when you will be up against a hard-nosed opponent and you'll have to use tough tactics yourself to avoid being victimized. In many cases, though, you'll be able to create a climate of trust and focus the discussion on the problem. When an adversary negotiation can be changed into a collaborative one, both sides usually come out better.

3.

Nice guys finish first

From the beginning of negotiations it's vital to remember that your ultimate success depends on persuasion. If you have the power to force people to do what you want, and you don't care whether they like it or not, why bother to negotiate? The reason people negotiate is to try to find a solution that is at least reasonably satisfactory to both sides.

Too many people approach a negotiation as if it were a court trial. They present all the evidence they can to make their opponents' proposals look bad and their own look good. But there isn't any impartial judge to award them the verdict on the basis of a preponderance of evidence. The parties to a negotiation are the judges, and there isn't going to be any decision at all unless they both agree to it.

That's why it pays to be a "nice guy" when you're negotiating. People are a lot more inclined to make concessions when they see you as a friendly human being—one whose attitude conveys understanding and respect, and concern for their feelings and needs.

Whatever position you take in a negotiation, do it like a nice guy. Nice guys don't like to disappoint people. They don't like to say no, to take unpopular positions, or to make demands that seem unreasonable. But they can do it just as well—and just as persistently—as a hard-nose, and create far less resentment in the process.

Nice guys don't claim that statements and statistics presented by their opponents are a bunch of lies. Instead, they listen, they make sure they understand what's been said, and they act a little puzzled. Then they present evidence that *seems* to contradict the statements. They sympathize with the needs and desires of their opponents. They are sincerely regretful when they have to take a conflicting position—but they take it and stick to it just the same.

When it comes to the point where somebody—perhaps both sides—have to make some concessions to reach an agreement, negotiators who have proved they are nice guys are more likely to receive and benefit from such concessions than those who haven't.

ADVICE FROM BEN FRANKLIN

Some thoughts on the art of negotiating, from Benjamin Franklin's *Autobiography*:

I made it a rule to forbear all direct contradictions to the sentiments of others, and all positive assertion of my own. I even forbade myself the use of every word or expression in the language that imported a fixed opinion, such as "certainly", "undoubtedly", etc. I adopted instead of them "I conceive", "I apprehend", or "I imagine" a thing to be so or so; or "so it appears to me at present".

When another asserted something that I thought an error, I denied myself the pleasure of contradicting him abruptly, and of showing immediately some absurdity in his proposition. In answering I began by observing that in certain cases or circumstances his opinion would be right, but in the present case there appeared or seemed to me some difference, etc.

I soon found the advantage of this change in my manner; the conversations I engaged in went on more pleasantly. The modest way in which I proposed my opinions procured them a readier reception and less contradiction. I had less mortification when I was found to be in the wrong, and I more easily prevailed with others to give up their mistakes and join with me when I happened to be in the right.

4.

Negotiation ethics

Most of us want to be fair and honest. We like to give a square deal and get a square deal. But there are some people who don't hesitate to indulge in "cheap tricks" to gain an advantage.

It isn't always possible to say what is ethical and what is unethical. There are gray areas where there can be honest disagreements. But there are some practices that almost all business negotiators would consider unethical. Here are some of them:

1. *Physical discomfort.* Some negotiators deliberately try to make their opponents uncomfortable. Typical practices include raising the thermostat in summer and lowering it in winter, positioning the opponent facing the sun or other glaring light, or providing a hard, uncomfortable chair for the opponent. The object is to make the opponent so uncomfortable that he or she will make concessions just to get the negotiations over with.

2. *False authorities.* An opponent may bring into the negotiating session "authorities" who are supposed to help prove a point. There is certainly nothing wrong with

bringing in genuine authorities, but it is clearly unethical to bring in individuals whose titles and qualifications have been falsified.

3. *Personal bribes or incentives.* Two purchasers for a large aerospace company were once offered a million dollars each in Swiss bank accounts for "seeing things our way". This is an extreme case, and easy to recognize. But bribery may also include such gratuities as free trips or expensive merchandise. Free lunches or dinners or inspection tours at the vendor's expense are usually not considered bribery; they may be a normal part of the business routine.

4. *False information.* Most opponents do not expect you to give away your company's secrets. Many negotiators refuse to answer as many questions as they answer. But it is unethical to deliberately present false and misleading information to deceive a negotiating opponent.

5. *False incentives.* "If you let us recoup some costs, we can do better next time." "If we get a good deal from you this time, we can give you twice the business next time." These are attractive incentives, but what if no such level of business really exists? What if things are really going to be worse on the next contract? Any promises beyond the agreement that are unlikely to be deliverable are unethical.

The more specific the false promise, the more unethical it is. A false promise to do "20 percent better next time" is more deceptive than a promise to "make every effort to do better next time".

6. *Half-truths and distorted statistics.* The misuse of information is another unethical practice. For example, suppose that this statement is made: "In one shipment, 50 percent of the units were defective." But what if the normal shipment is 1000 units, and the shipment in question was a sample shipment of only two units? Such a statement is a half-truth and a distortion of reality.

7. *False records.* Some negotiating opponents will go so far as to present false data, phony testimonials, bogus test results, or biased lab reports to support their statements. Such practices are both unethical *and* illegal.

Responding to unethical tactics

What do you do when you discover an unethical practice? It is not always necessary to break off negotiations and dismiss the offender permanently. The situation requires some analysis of the seriousness of the offense and the offender's intentions and motives.

If the infraction is minor, such as turning off the air conditioner in the summer, it is probably best simply to say that you are uncomfortable and would like to move to more comfortable facilities or adjourn until the problem can be corrected. Calling the bluff is usually sufficient to correct the problem and to discourage the opponent from trying anything of that nature again.

If the infraction is more serious, more consideration is necessary. Assume, for instance, that you learn that your negotiating opponent has obtained confidential information by the use of some kind of spy system. If there are good alternatives to dealing with the offender, it is probably best to terminate the negotiations altogether and take your business elsewhere. But if there is nowhere else to turn, your next strategy should be to confront the opponents and expose them.

Most opponents who have been caught cheating will be embarrassed enough for you to hold a temporary advantage and gain concessions. You may also pose the threat of legal action or threaten to report them to a regulatory agency.

In general, it simply isn't wise or necessary to deal with unethical opponents. If the negotiations involve long-term relationships between the parties, you can infer that an opponent who is unethical or dishonest during negotiations will be equally dishonest during the entire life of the agreement. If so, the final cost of the agreement may turn out to be much more than you estimated. In the long run, it's better to look for other sources to deal with—people who have a reputation for fair, honest dealings and don't need trickery to insure that things turn out favorably for them.

5.

Power and leverage

The outcome of any negotiation is strongly influenced by the relative power of the two parties. Power in negotiations has been defined as the ability to influence the behavior of an opponent. The negotiator who is in the strongest position will usually come out with the better deal.

The truth of these statements is so obvious that people faced with negotiation opponents who are apparently in a strong bargaining position often throw up their hands and settle for much less than they should. They don't realize that careful preparation for a negotiation can change the power balance in their favor.

Power is not an absolute thing. It is always relative. No party in a negotiation—no buyer or seller—ever enjoys complete power over the other party.

In a negotiation, power is subjective—it's all in the mind. If you're absolutely desperate to buy someone's collection of bottlecaps, but he doesn't know how urgently you want it, he has gained no power. If you're negotiating with a contractor for a home-improvement job that he needs badly, and you don't know about his need, you have no advantage. Power is power only when it is *perceived* as power by both parties in the negotiation.

Before starting to negotiate with anyone, therefore, determine just what kinds of power you have and what your opponent has. Look around and try to find other sources of leverage that will give you an advantage. Then be sure that the other person is aware of the strength of your bargaining position.

Here are some common kinds of leverage that negotiators have found valuable in the past.

Acceptable alternatives

If you can't get what you want out of these negotiations, what alternatives are available to you? And what alternatives are available to your opponent?

The more good alternatives you have—and the fewer that are available to your opponent—the more leverage you can bring to bear. Convincing your opponent that there is competition—that you can find a suitable solution elsewhere—gives you extra leverage to get the kind of agreement you want.

If you have no alternatives—and if your opponent knows this—your negotiation leverage is greatly reduced, especially if you need to make a deal. If you're trying to sell your house and no one has expressed an interest in buying it, you'll have a hard time trying to negotiate a high price with a potential buyer. But if even three or four other people are interested in the house, the potential buyer will feel much more pressure to increase his offer.

This boils down to two basic rules of thumb: (1) If you're buying something, get as many people as possible to compete for your business, and (2) if you're selling something, line up as many potential customers as possible. In both cases, you increase your leverage by raising doubts in your opponent's mind about your willingness to make concessions during the negotiation. The more competitors you can show to your opponent, the greater will be your negotiating leverage.

Using influence

Gather as much support as possible for your proposal before beginning the negotiation. The more support you have from people who might have an influence on the other person, the greater the leverage you will have.

Suppose, for example, that you're proposing a new product or a new course of action to your boss. The first question the boss is likely to ask is, "Have you discussed this idea with anyone else?"

If your answer is, "No, I haven't," you may not have lost any ground, but you haven't gained any support for your position, either. If your answer is, "Yes, I did, but none of them thought much of it," you've obviously lost some leverage; you'll have to overcome the effect of the negative opinions before you can make any headway. But if you can say, "Yes, I've discussed it with everyone in the department and several other executives, and they all think that it has great potential"—the boss is going to have to give the idea serious consideration.

Backing from upstairs

Your leverage is enhanced when you can count on solid support from those you represent; it's weakened when you can't. If the person you're dealing with becomes dissatisfied with the way things are going, he or she may try to go over your head and deal with your boss. If you have obtained the solid backing of the boss before the negotiation, your opponent will run into a stone wall and be forced to deal with you. By reducing the number of alternatives available to your opponent, you diminish the amount of leverage that can be used against you.

Need for the deal

The person who needs the deal most has the least leverage in a negotiation—if the other person is aware of that need.

If you want to get your air conditioner repaired, you'll be in a far better position to negotiate a favorable arrangement with the local service company if you call them in the early spring, before the hot weather sets in. At that point, you're experiencing no discomfort and you have no pressing need to have the air conditioner fixed. The service company, on the other hand, is in a slow period and may desperately need your business.

In the middle of August, the situation is reversed. Now the service firm has all the business it can handle, and you need the deal more than they do.

This kind of leverage is present in most negotiations. Suppliers find purchasing agents far easier to negotiate with when they are about to run out of a needed material. Purchasing agents find that suppliers will make more concessions when customers have been hard to find and salespeople are failing to meet their quotas.

Before you negotiate with anyone, try to determine who has the most leverage—who needs the deal least. Ask yourself: How much do I need the other party? How much does the other party need me? How much do we need each other?

If your investigation indicates that your opponent needs the deal more than you do, you can capitalize on that. If you find that you need the deal more than your opponent, plan to do what you can to disguise this fact and try to find some acceptable alternatives before you start negotiating.

WHO NEEDS THE DEAL MOST?

Negotiators who can accurately assess their opponents' needs and pressures chalk up some amazing success stories.

A newly organized management consulting partnership was looking to land its first big, long-term consulting contract. The two partners were negotiating with a prospective client to provide 60 days of consulting time per year over a period of eight years.

Since the job was so substantial, the partners were determined not to let it get away. They assumed that the job was so desirable that many consultants would be bidding on it, so they decided to reduce their regular daily fee by 25 percent to insure that they would be competitive.

Before making the trip to the client's headquarters, one of the partners called the client's secretary to verify the meeting arrangements. During the conversation, he casually asked whether any other consultants had worked on the project in the past. Yes, she told him, another consulting team had been brought in, but their work was less than satisfactory and they had been let go. That, she told him, was why the corporate staff were under pressure from upstairs to get a replacement without delay.

In the light of this information, the partners reconsidered their bargaining position. The potential client didn't know how much they wanted the assignment, but they knew that the client was under pressure to reach a quick agreement. They had leverage that they weren't aware of before. After some discussion, they decided that they could probably raise their usual fee by 50 percent and still have a good chance of landing the job.

The meeting with the potential client went smoothly, and the client's representatives seemed satisfied that the consultants would do a good job. When the question of fees came up, the partner doing the talking wavered. He was tempted to quote a reduced fee to insure that they got the job. His pulse quickened, his palms were sweating, and he was sure his voice would quaver, but he stuck with the strategy and quoted a fee that was 50 percent higher than usual.

Fortunately, the consultants' analysis of the situation proved correct. After only a brief discussion, the client's representatives accepted the fee. Later, one of them said to the consultants, "We ordinarily don't pay consultants that much. You guys must have known you were the only ones being considered."

If the consultants hadn't utilized the leverage that was theirs, they would have left half of the fee they actually received lying on the bargaining table.

6.

The time element

Time is one of the major factors that influence the outcome of any negotiation. More concessions are made in the eleventh hour of a negotiating session than in all the preceding negotiating time. The existence of a deadline almost always produces a last-ditch effort by both parties to reach an agreement.

Of course, if the deadline is an arbitrary one—when, for example, both sides have agreed to conclude the negotiation at a certain time—there will be no great pressure to meet it. But when one or both parties face costly consequences if the deadline is not met, the chances of reaching an agreement are much greater.

The party that is most constrained by time limits is in a weaker position and will invariably give up more as the deadline approaches. If the consequences of not meeting the deadline are serious to both parties—as, for example, in many labor negotiations prior to a strike deadline—both sides will feel it necessary to make concessions. But if the consequences are greater for one party than for the other, the outcome will be lopsided. If, for example, a buyer has a production schedule to meet and the seller has no rigid deadline, the buyer will usually have to make greater concessions to close the deal.

Deadlines—theirs and ours

In adversary negotiations, you are at an advantage if you know your opponents' deadlines. If you know that a seller must get an order that day, for example, you can be more insistent that your terms be met. If, on the other hand, your opponents know your deadline, you are at a disadvantage. They can draw out the negotiation until your deadline is almost at hand, putting great pressure on you to give away more than you'd like to.

Obviously, then, it makes good sense to try to find out what your opponents' real deadlines are. And it's good strategy, whenever possible, not to reveal your deadlines to the other side.

Many of us go into negotiations with a self-imposed handicap. We are very much aware of the deadline we have to meet, and this puts pressure on us to make concessions in order to close a deal before the time runs out. It's wise to keep in mind that the other side has time pressures too. They may appear calm, cool, and collected, unconcerned by the passing of time. But almost always they have deadlines of their own, and beneath the surface they may be just as anxious as you are to reach an agreement.

It's also a good idea to take a good look at your deadline to see whether it's as hard-and-fast as it seems. Most deadlines are more flexible than you might think. There are times when it really is vital to meet a particular deadline, but in most cases the world won't come to an end if a specific deadline isn't met. This doesn't mean that you should ignore deadlines, but you should analyze them to determine how firm and how important they really are.

Ask yourself: Is this deadline real, or is it one I've imposed on myself? If necessary, can I negotiate an extension with the other party or with my own organization? What will happen if I don't meet the deadline? How serious will the consequences be? What is the likelihood that these consequences will really occur? In other words, just how great is the risk I'm taking?

Answering questions like these can put the importance of your deadline in perspective. It can help you to determine how much pressure you're really under and to what extent you're making it needlessly difficult for yourself to negotiate. Time limits have a way of intimidating us; unless we question them, we tend to accept them unthinkingly. If you don't think that's true, take a look at the front desk of a hotel at checkout time. You'll see a long line of people trying to meet the checkout deadline that the hotel has posted on their doors, no matter how inconvenient it may be for them. If you were one of those people, you might ask yourself: what's the reason for a one o'clock checkout time? (Because the cleaning people have to change the sheets and get the room ready for the next guests.) Will all the rooms be cleaned at the stroke of one? (Of course not; some won't be touched for hours.) Then if I want to keep my things in the room a little longer, can't I negotiate a later checkout time with the manager? (Almost certainly, you can.)

Creating deadlines for others

Because deadlines do tend to be intimidating, you can often spur your negotiating opponents to action by creating deadlines for them. If you can give them a deadline that is credible, they'll have a strong incentive to move quickly to reach an agreement before time runs out.

When you're in the position of the seller in a negotiation, you may find deadlines like these will help the other party make the decision you want:

—This offer is good only until July 15.

—If I don't have your order by March 1, I won't be able to deliver by March 31.

—If we don't get your deposit by Thursday, we won't be able to hold it for you.

—The price is going up on May 15.

—It will take our plant six weeks to produce an order this size.

When you're the buyer in a negotiation, you can also create deadlines for the seller. Salespeople sometimes welcome having a deadline; it helps them negotiate with their own management to get an okay to close the deal. Here are some examples of deadlines that can get a seller moving:

—My boss has to approve this purchase, and he's going on vacation Friday.

—We aren't accepting bids after September 1.

—Our fiscal year ends April 30; I have to make this purchase before then.

—I need a price by tomorrow.

—If we can't agree by Wednesday, I'll have to talk to your competitor.

In many negotiations, you can create deadlines of this kind. They can be a help in getting action from the other party.

Pacing the negotiation

Because most of the movement and most of the concessions in a negotiation occur when the deadline is imminent, it's a good idea to save the issues that are most important to you for the end of the negotiation. The other side is likely to become much more flexible as the deadline nears.

But you shouldn't surprise your negotiating opponents with a large demand at the last minute. If, for example, you're going to ask for a price that's a good deal higher than they were originally intending to pay, they will need time to adjust to the idea. It takes time for people to adjust their thinking to anything new, different, or unexpected. Buyers need time to accept the fact that they're going to have to pay more than they had planned. Sellers need time to adjust their unrealistic price expectations downward. People can't accept new and unpleasant realities immediately.

It's best, therefore, to state the positions that are important to you, but that may come as something of a shock to the other party, fairly early in the negotiation. Talk about them, but don't try to reach an agreement immediately. Put them off until later, and go on to settle other, less important differences first. When you then bring up your demands again at the end of the negotiation, your negotiating opponents will have had time to become accustomed to them and will be less likely to reject them out of hand.

Pacing the negotiation in this way has another extremely important advantage. By the time you reach the issues that are most critical in your eyes, your negotiating opponents will have invested a great deal of time and energy in the negotiation. You will have already reached agreement on a number of other issues, and all that remains to be settled are the points that are most important to you.

Under these circumstances, your opponents are much more likely to be flexible in making concessions. Having come this far, they will be reluctant to write off all the time and energy they have already invested and start all over again with someone else, who may be even more difficult to deal with than you.

It's a good general rule: Whenever you have an important issue to negotiate, don't try to reach an agreement until late in the negotiation, when your opponents will have invested so much time and energy that it will be more attractive for them to make concessions than to break off the negotiations.

Part II.

The Negotiating Process

7.

Preparing to negotiate

If you want to buy 100 shares of General Motors stock, the procedure is relatively simple. You call your broker, find out the current price, and place your order. You don't expect to pay less than the market price, and you certainly won't pay more. It's a straightforward transaction, and no negotiations are involved.

A negotiating situation is a good deal more complicated. Each party in a negotiation must have something the other wants. There must be an "acceptance range" between their two positions, and both parties must be prepared to make some concessions to reach a compromise within that range—a settlement that allows both of them to walk away feeling that they have won something.

Reaching an agreement is going to take a lot of explaining, educating, and bargaining, so you have to be prepared in advance. The more thoroughly you prepare, the better the outcome is likely to be. Hasty decisions, not considered in advance, are often bad decisions.

Know thyself

To begin with, you have to know exactly what you want from the negotiation. From your point of view, what is the optimum solution? What is the minimum solution you are prepared to accept? What factors are unimportant to you so you're willing to concede them? What will you reluctantly concede, if necessary, to reach your primary objective? And what do you consider nonnegotiable?

Obviously, things like this have to be considered sometime. If you think them over first, carefully and thoroughly, you'll be less likely to be pushed into a bad decision during the negotiation.

Know your opponent

You should also learn everything you can about the person you'll be negotiating with. If it's a buying or selling situation, information on such things as your opponent's financial condition, inventory levels, and competitive situation will help you determine how strong your opponent's bargaining position will be and how you can best present your case.

In addition to the facts and figures, you are most interested in learning the real needs of your opponent. These needs may not be apparent; in fact, your opponent may not want you to know what they are, if that knowledge will give you a negotiating advantage. But the more you know about them, the better you will be able to plan your negotiating strategy.

How badly does your opponent need to reach an agreement? How badly does he need to reach an agreement with *you*? What kind of time pressure is he under? What does he know about *your* goals and *your* need to reach an agreement?

How do you get this kind of information? Depending on the situation, some of it may be available in public sources. Financial information can be obtained from Dun and Bradstreet reports, credit checks, and stockholder reports. Such things as legal judgments, contract awards, mortgages, and liens are available from public records. Newspapers, trade publications, and professional associations can be sources of information.

Talk informally with anyone who might be able to help you—people who work with or for your opponent, friends and associates, secretaries, staff people. Third-party sources can often be helpful—customers, past customers, suppliers. Anyone who has dealt with your opponent may be able to provide information that will be of value to you.

When you determine what your opponent wants and needs, you'll be in a position to consider alternate strategies and pick the one that has the highest probability of accomplishing your goals.

Making an agenda

Before the meeting, prepare an agenda listing all the points you want to bring out during the negotiation. For informal negotiations, this can be a simple checklist of topics you don't want to overlook, points you want to cover, and objectives you want to reach. While doing this, you can decide how and when you want to introduce the various issues. This will help you to keep the initiative and structure the negotiation to your best advantage.

NOT ENOUGH HOMEWORK

A young lawyer was given the job of buying a building for his client. Because of depressed business conditions in the area, there were many buildings available, and the lawyer easily found one that would suit his client's purposes. In fact, when his client saw it, he was delighted.

When it came time for negotiations, the lawyer was careful not to tip his hand. He was certain the seller had no inkling of his client's enthusiasm for the property.

The client's financial people estimated the building's worth at about $600,000, but the lawyer was sure he could get it for less. Upon checking with several real estate friends, he found that comparable buildings had recently sold for about $500,000 because of the depressed market. Finally, after careful negotiating, he was able to get it for $425,000 because of his client's willingness to pay cash. Needless to say, the client was overjoyed.

It wasn't until a year later at a cocktail party that the lawyer learned the truth: The seller would have been willing to go as low as $300,000 for a cash deal, because they were cash-strapped and needed every penny just to survive.

The lawyer shrugged his shoulders. "Inside information," he said. "How was I to know?"

"Simple," said his informant. "It was in the business section of several newspapers that the firm was liquidating its assets for cash as rapidly as possible. They were sure you had read about it, and they were hoping they could still get the $300,000. After they closed the deal with you, they celebrated for two days . . . . Don't you read the papers?"

8.

Planning a defense

When you're preparing to negotiate, you try to find out as much as you can about your opponent's goals, needs, deadlines, and any other pressures or influences that will give you a better idea of how to approach the negotiation. It's well to remember that your opponent is trying to find out the same things about you.

As part of your preparations, review the problem areas that your opponent might try to exploit. Where are you vulnerable? How badly do you need to reach an agreement? Do you have any deadlines that have to be met?

Which of your weaknesses might your opponent be aware of? What impact could this knowledge have on the negotiation? In what way could your opponent use your weaknesses to gain an advantage?

Answering these questions before the negotiation gives you time to think about your vulnerabilities and prepare to avoid or minimize the harmful effects they might cause. Don't trust to luck or rely on your native genius to come up with the right response on the spur of the moment. Think things through in advance, and come up with some plausible ways to disguise or minimize your weaknesses.

Handling tough questions

During the negotiation, your opponent will be probing for your vulnerabilities. Questions will be asked that you don't want to answer—or at least you don't want to answer too early in the negotiation. If you identify these questions before you begin, you'll be able to prepare to handle them.

The following tactics can help you deal with tough questions. Think each question through and decide which tactic would be most appropriate for handling it.

1. *Rephrase the question.* If you don't want to answer a question as it is posed, you may be able to reinterpret it and alter it into a form that you are willing to answer. Then you can restate the question your way, using an opening phrase like, "I think what you are really asking is . . . ." But be sure you answer enough of the question so that your opponent doesn't come back and bluntly repeat the same question.

2. *Play dumb.* Sometimes you can get away with simply saying that you don't know the answer. If the question is important to the outcome of the negotiation, you'll probably have to answer it sooner or later, but many questions are not relevant and are asked only to build your opponent's position.

3. *Defer the question until later.* Many questions can be deferred by claiming the need for additional thought

or more information, or the necessity to consult with someone else. You can put off the questioner by saying something like, "I can't answer that question right now;

TURNING THE TABLES

Margaret Karsh was a buyer for a consumer products company. Her immediate problem was to purchase customized packaging for a new product that was to be introduced nationally by an advertising campaign scheduled to begin on March 15. The new product had to be packaged and delivered to retail establishments across the country prior to that date.

To maintain her leverage in price negotiations, Margaret did not want her packaging suppliers to find out about that March 15 deadline. She realized, of course, that all of them knew that the packaging was for a new product. Since new product introductions usually involve crash programs to get the product to the retail shelves on time, it was highly likely that the packaging suppliers with whom she would be negotiating would try to determine and exploit her deadline.

In her defensive planning, therefore, Margaret developed a convincing response to any questions about her deadline. When a supplier's representative suggested that she

I'll have to check with_____and get back to you." The additional time you gain will enable you to formulate the best possible answer. Sometimes the

---

would have to pay a higher price to get the the packages produced on a rush basis, Margaret told him: "Well, the company isn't exactly sure when the new product will be introduced. What we want to do is purchase the packaging and put it into inventory, so we'll be ready to go when management decides that the time is right."

Margaret then reached into her drawer and took out a clipping from a national business magazine. She showed it to the representative and said, "I thought this would be a good time to get started, since there seems to be a good deal of excess capacity out there right now and a lot of suppliers will be able to do the job." The clipping was an article stating that orders for this kind of packaging had declined for the seventh straight month.

In this way, Margaret succeeded in taking the focus off *her* problem—the deadline— and focused the representative's attention on *his* problem—the fact that his company needed the business. This put her in an excellent bargaining position and enabled her to reach an advantageous agreement on prices and delivery.

question will be forgotten altogether. In this case, unless the answer enhances your position, you need not raise the issue again yourself.

4. *Counter with your own question.* Use a phrase like, "I'm sorry, but I can't answer that question until you tell me . . . ." This puts your opponent on the defensive. He or she may rephrase or tone down the question, or withdraw it altogether. If the opponent does answer your question, and if you still don't want to reply, you can use another of these tactics to defer your response.

5. *Give a qualified answer.* Almost any answer can be qualified by some sort of disclaimer, such as:

"Well, subject to the approval of . . ."

"Assuming nothing else changes . . ."

"Provided we can conclude the agreement on this note . . ."

"Depending on what we find when we take a closer look . . ."

Such qualifiers leave the door open for you to change your mind in the future.

6. *Split the answer.* When a yes or no answer is requested, you can often say that the answer could be either yes *or* no. Then go on to explain the circumstances that could affect the answer or the concessions necessary before you are willing to commit to an unfavorable position.

7. *Argue with the question.* You can challenge some questions by saying something like, "I don't really think

that's the right question. Can you restate it in terms of . . . ." This may cause your opponent to change the question, to break it down, or to put it in a form that you're willing to deal with.

It's also possible to say that you don't understand the question, to ask that the question be broken down into parts, or to claim that you simply don't see the relevancy of the question to the discussion.

This list doesn't include every response that can be made to a question you don't want to answer, but it does contain some proven solutions.

In general, you shouldn't duck or defer questions unless you have a good reason. Whenever possible, it's best to answer the questions when they are asked. This requires advance preparation of answers to tough questions that you expect to come up in the negotiation, but it almost always puts you in a stronger position than answering questions on a deferred basis or in an altered form.

9.

The opening offer

Any negotiation has to begin with the parties stating their positions. In labor-management negotiations, the union makes its demands and management sets forth what it will offer. In price negotiations, the selling party states the price it wants to receive and the buying party states how much it is willing to pay. In interpersonal negotiations, each party explains what he or she wants the other to do or to agree to.

The opening position you take is important, because you know that you're never going to get more (or give less) than your opening offer. But there are many uncertainties involved. Should you make the first offer, or should you let the other person make the first move? How much below what you're willing to pay should your offer be? Or how much above what you're willing to accept should you ask for?

Who makes the first offer?

There are situations in which it is advantageous for you to get your offer on the table first. There are other situations in which it is in your best interest to hold back and let your opponent make the first offer.

In general, there are two kinds of situations in which it will be to your advantage to make the opening offer.

1. *When you want to take charge of the negotiation.* The more you know about the situation—your own wants, needs, strengths, and weaknesses, as well as those of your opponent—the more advantageous it is for you to make the first offer. By doing so, you select the point at which the negotiation will begin. You save the time and effort involved in starting at a point determined by the other party and having to struggle to move the negotiation to a point near your own realistic goal.

2. *When you want to soften the opposition.* Negotiation opponents often become more receptive to your position if they are given some time to think it over and get accustomed to it. Stating your position immediately gives them more time to think it over and get used to it. It also makes it clear to them at the outset that they should not have any unrealistic expectations about the outcome of the negotiation.

Situations in which you may want to *avoid* making the opening offer include the following:

1. *When you're not sure of your opponents' interests and positions.* If you're not sure where your opponents are coming from or what they're after, it's usually best to keep your own position to yourself and let them make the opening offer. They may make an offer that's better than what you had initially hoped for. Even if they don't, at least you'll know where they stand.

2. *When you need time to probe for more information.*
By getting your opponents to lay an offer on the table and
defend it, you buy time to get additional information. By
holding back your opening position and asking your
opponents questions about their offer, you can determine
how interested they are in doing business and how badly
they want to make a deal.

Determining your opening offer

Your opening offer has an extremely important effect
on the success of any negotiation. You're probably going
to have to settle for less than you ask for, but it's certain
that you won't get *more* than you ask for. That's why the
people who get the best results in negotiations are those
who initially set their sights high.

University studies have verified that negotiators with
higher expectations get higher settlements. Negotiators
who expect less are willing to settle for less. In one experi-
ment involving 120 professional negotiatiors, those with
high aspirations were winners in every case in which
they faced opponents with low aspirations—even when
they were less skilled and operating from a weaker
bargaining position.

Successful negotiators usually begin with the toughest
opening offer they can reasonably justify. If they're
buying, they offer a very low price. If they're selling, they
ask a very high price.

This has the immediate effect of undermining the
opponent's confidence in his or her starting position. If

your opening offer is credible, it reduces the opponent's expectations about the likely outcome of the negotiation.

To have the desired effect, however, your opening offer must be *credible*. You can't just pull a figure out of a hat and expect to be taken seriously. If you offer a man $200 for his $20,000 sports car, he will rightfully consider the offer too frivolous even to discuss. But if you offer $15,000, pointing out that you will have to spend a good deal of money to put it into proper shape, he may be convinced, however reluctantly, that your offer must form the basis for the negotiation.

There is a certain amount of risk in this approach, of course. If you're dealing with someone whose aspiration level is as high as your own, there's a good possibility of a deadlock. In the long run, though, you'll be far more successful in your negotiations if you keep your aspiration level realistically high.

YOU GOTTA BELIEVE!

Before you can become committed to a negotiation goal, you must fully believe that the goal is not only justified but attainable. If you aren't convinced that it is attainable, you aren't likely to achieve it. You may enter negotiations with high hopes and the best of intentions, but you will easily fall prey to opponents who are more committed to their positions.

Janet Wiley was the head of the word-processing department in a small eastern company. Her husband Ken was being sent by his company on a business trip to San Francisco—a city Janet had always wanted to visit. "Why don't you come with me?" Ken said. "I can wrap up my business in a week, then we'll take a week to see the town. As long as we travel together, you can fly for half fare."

The rub was that Janet had used all but one week of her vacation, and she wasn't sure she could get a week's leave of absence to make the trip. "You know Mr. Crane," a friend at the office said to her. "He doesn't approve of leaves of absence, even without pay." Janet knew that, but she decided it was worth a try.

"I'm sorry, Janet," Mr. Crane said when Janet had made her request. "I'd like to help you, but you know our policy—no leaves of absence except for emergency situations. And a trip to San Francisco is hardly an emergency."

Janet took her trip—but only for one week. A week after Ken left, she flew out to join him—at full fare. Had she been more convinced that her goal was justified and attainable, she might have made out much better.

Because she wasn't totally convinced that her goal was within reason, she had developed no ammunition to support her position. She could have pointed out the importance of the trip to her, and told Mr. Crane that she had trained her people to operate independently in her absence. She could have reminded him that things ran smoothly when she was away for two weeks on her last vacation. She could have told him that Ed Williams, who had held her job before he was promoted, had promised to look in on the department to make sure no problems would develop. Policies are not carved in stone, and some are quite arbitrary. If she had been more strongly committed to her position, she could have developed arguments that undoubtedly would have convinced her boss. Lacking commitment, she settled for less than she probably could have won.

10.

Making concessions

In any negotiation, both parties have some room to give. That's what makes it a negotiation, rather than a "take it or leave it" proposition. Your goal is to give away as little as possible in order to make a deal.

Here are some guidelines for making—and getting—concessions during the give-and-take of negotiations.

Never give something for nothing

This is probably the most important single principle of negotiating. Giving up something without getting something in return will not make your opponent more generous; in fact, the contrary is true.

There are quite a few people who believe that if they make one or two "goodwill" concessions, they will "soften up" their opponents by this show of generosity. But generosity is not contagious. Most negotiators will gladly accept anything you give them for nothing, but they will feel no obligation to reciprocate.

Goodwill concessions actually have the opposite effect: They are most likely to be seen as a sign of weakness, and the expectations of your opponents will be raised. Research findings—and practical experience—confirm the fact that rather than softening up the other side, goodwill concessions make them tougher. If you are willing to give them something for nothing, how much more will they be able to get when the real bargaining begins?

Giving up a concession without receiving anything in return simply moves you closer to your opponent's position and narrows the range in which you can negotiate. Never concede anything without getting something back—preferably more than you've given.

Keep concessions small and infrequent

Giving large concessions to negotiating opponents has much the same effect as giving away something for nothing. It raises their expectations and encourages them to press you to go further than you want to. It indicates to your opponent that your initial offer wasn't really serious. It suggests that you are not in a strong position and that you can be pressured into further concessions.

The timing of concessions also has an effect on the outcome of the negotiation. Research has shown that the first party to make a major concession usually comes out on the short end of the final settlement. And negotiators who make concessions at a regular rate encourage their opponents to keep the negotiation going and wait for more.

In short, avoid making the first major concession, and keep the concessions you do make small and infrequent whenever possible.

Make concessions progressively smaller

Your first concession shouldn't be large, but it should be the largest one you make. After that, each additional concession should be progressively smaller.

Suppose you want to sell an item for $10, and the person you're negotiating with has offered to pay $7.50. How much of the $2.50 difference will you have to compromise?

Chances are, your final settlement will depend on how big a concession you start with. If you lower your price to $9, your opponent will probably be able to get another dollar or so in concessions, winding up with the lion's share of the original difference. Suppose, however, that your first offer is to cut the price by 25 cents. This won't make your opponent very happy, but it gives you much more room to make further concessions if necessary.

If each concession you make is the same or larger, you encourage your opponent to simply wait you out. Instead, make your second concession 20 cents, the third 15 cents, and so on. These progressively smaller concessions indicate to your opponent that you are getting down to your rock-bottom price. Creating this impression helps insure that the settlement will be in your favor.

Sell your concessions

People don't appreciate things that they get too easily. They tend to assume that they really aren't worth much.

Before you make a concession, therefore, use a little "sell" to make sure that your opponent realizes that it's really valuable. Point out how much it's worth. Think out loud about how much it will cost or inconvenience you. Before you decide to give away anything, be sure your opponent appreciates it.

CHARLIE'S CAR

Charlie Ryan got off the commuter train and turned up his collar against the cold wind. "I've put it off long enough," he said to himself. "I've got to get a station car. It's getting too cold to walk to and from the station every day."

As he crossed the parking lot, he saw an older model car with a For Sale sign in the side window. The used cars Charlie had seen advertised all cost more money than he wanted to spend, but this one didn't look very expensive. As he was looking it over, a man approached the car.

"Your car?" Charlie asked.

"That's right," the man said.

"I've been looking for a station car," Charlie said. "How does this run?"

"Runs like a charm," the man said. "I know it's not the greatest looking car in the world, but mechanically it's perfect. I always took good care of the engine."

"Well," Charlie said, "I'm not interested in looks. I just want dependable transportation. What are you asking for it?"

"As a matter of fact, I'm not sure," the man said. "I just decided to sell it, and I didn't get a chance to check to find out what it's worth."

"I'll tell you what," Charlie said. "If it really runs well, I'll give you $300 for it."

"It runs fine," the man said, "but I want to check before I set a price."

"Maybe $300 is a little low," Charlie said. "Will you take $400?"

"Gee, I don't know," the man said. "It may be worth more than that."

"Look," Charlie said. "I really need a car. I don't want to pay an arm and a leg, but I'm willing to be reasonable. How about $500— cash?"

"I want to be reasonable, too," the man said. "It's just that I don't want to lose money on the deal."

By now Charlie had convinced himself that this was the car he wanted and that he wouldn't be able to get a better bargain anywhere else. "Okay," he said. "I'll make it

$600. But that's my final offer—take it or leave it."

The man thought for a moment. "Well," he said, "I guess that sounds fair. Okay, it's a deal."

As the man had said, the car ran very well, and Charlie was quite pleased with his purchase. Pleased, that is, until one day he happened to see the identical model in a used car lot. It was priced for sale at $275.

And that's how Charlie found out that he had a lot to learn about negotiating. He had made every mistake in the book: He hadn't done his homework, so he didn't know how much the car was really worth. He made concessions without getting anything in return. He raised the owner's expectations by appearing anxious to reach an agreement and by making large, regular concessions. In short, he talked himself into paying twice what he probably could have bought the car for.

11.

Changing the package

When negotiations drag on and on without resolution, you eventually have to decide whether or not they're worth continuing. The issues have been laid out and negotiated to the point where both sides are unwilling to grant any further concessions. The discussion has degenerated into a rehash of positions.

When it is clear that there is no middle ground, for all practical purposes, the negotiations are over. In commercial negotiations, this is not an unusual situation. Buyers and sellers frequently reject each other's proposal on the assumption that other, more acceptable alternatives are available to them. In some cases, you may decide that what you stand to gain isn't worth the time and effort necessary to pursue an agreement further.

Breaking off negotiations calls for tact. Who knows what tomorrow may bring? If you part politely, without aggravating any bad feelings, there may be some way you'll get back together again—next week, next month, or next year—in a mutually profitable arrangement. Times change; keep what friends you can and don't make enemies you don't have to.

When you make your last proposal, don't say, "This is it. Take it or leave it!" There's something offensive about those words and that attitude. Instead, put it in a tactful manner. You might say something like this: "We've thought it over carefully. We've tried to do the best we can to meet your needs and desires. I'm afraid, though, that this is the best we can do. I'm sorry if we can't make a deal favorable to both of us. If our situation changes, we'll be in touch with you. I hope you'll keep in touch with us."

No one is happy when a negotiation reaches an impasse; both sides are disappointed and frustrated. Try to part on as courteous a note as possible, and leave the door open for future dealings.

The "what if" approach

Many negotiations break down unnecessarily. It's possible for an agreement to be reached that benefits both parties, but they become stuck on one issue and deadlock because of it. With a little ingenuity, many of these deadlocks could be avoided.

There is almost always more than one variable in any proposal that is being negotiated. Price is usually the sticking point, but few deals are decided solely on the basis of price. There may be payment terms, delivery requirements, specifications, quality considerations, order sizes, repeat business, and any number of variables that can be adjusted to create an agreement satisfactory to both parties.

The key is to consider all these variables a package that can be changed by changing the size or shape of the elements in it. And the approach is to be flexible and question how the variables might be adjusted to create a mutually acceptable package. You can do this by asking "what if" questions. What if we accept a smaller down payment? What if we change the specifications? What if we agree to buy more than one? What if we provide a warranty?

For each change you agree to make in one variable, you expect a change in another variable in return. If we reduce the price by X amount, will you order a larger quantity? If we agree to pay this price, will you include a service contract? If we agree to buy your entire output, will you warehouse the material for us?

This approach helps create a climate in which new alternatives can be explored until a new package that benefits both parties is created.

Reviewing the variables

Before any negotiation, look at the proposition you intend to make and determine how many variables there really are. Don't just assume that some things are non-negotiable. Examine each part of the package with an eye to seeing what might be changed if necessary to reach an agreement. The more negotiable variables you have, the better your ability to repackage a deal so it is acceptable to both parties.

With *money*, for example, ask yourself: Can we change the number of payments? The down payment? The credit terms? Discounts for early payments? With *time*, ask yourself: Can the initial delivery date be changed? Can we produce this during our slack period? What constitutes late delivery? How long can we have to fulfill this contract?

By questioning each of the variables in the package, you will be able to come up with a number of negotiable variables that will give you the flexibility to trade off concessions with your opponents and put together a package that will be to the advantage of both parties.

12.

Closing the deal

Sooner or later, every negotiation session must come to an end. If the negotiation has gone smoothly, the negotiation will end naturally when both parties are satisfied with the resolution of all the issues in dispute. In many cases, though, you will feel satisfied that you've achieved your major goals and be ready to make a deal, but the other party will still show a lingering reluctance to reach a final agreement.

For situations like these, successful negotiators have developed a variety of techniques that can be useful in prodding a reluctant opponent into agreeing to close the deal.

Closing tactics

One of these closing tactics is designed to dispense with the necessity of long-drawn-out negotiating on a variety of minor issues. It calls for putting all the remaining issues on the table and presenting an overall final offer that ties them all into one cohesive package. If the package seems fair and the hour is late, the opponent is likely to accept it.

The "inducement" close offers a special concession for wrapping the deal up—right now. A typical offer might go something like this: "If we can have your signature now, we can. . . ." The implication is that if your opponent passes up this limited-time offer, it will be withdrawn forever. If your concession is valuable to your opponent, this approach may be enough to encourage him to close the deal.

There's some danger in using this tactic, however. If the concession you offer is not really time-bound, your opponent may refuse the deal, but may continue to demand the concession that you have already indicated was available.

The reverse of the "inducement" close could be called the "all-inclusive" close. Here you attempt to use the *acceptance* of a demand as leverage for closing the deal, For example: "If that's all it will take to close this deal, then we accept." It should be made clear that your acceptance of the request is contingent upon the conclusion of a final agreement.

Another closing tactic calls for taking some kind of physical action in anticipation of the close, such as starting to write up an order, gathering your papers together, standing up to shake hands with your opponent, or telephoning someone to report that the negotiation is about to conclude. Actions like these indicate that you consider the matter settled, and they can prod an indecisive opponent into agreeing to close.

The piecemeal closing

When the negotiations are fairly complex, the "piece-meal" closing tactic may be useful. It involves stopping to write an agreed-upon agenda for the rest of the negotiating session. The object is to list all the barriers or issues that stand in the way of an agreement, then proceed to check them off, one at a time, as they are agreed upon. This tactic can be effective when the issues have all been brought forward, but nothing seems to be happening. It's a way of getting things moving toward a final agreement.

Timing the close

The time to move for a close is after the major issues have been settled and only some minor ones stand in the way of an agreement. It's obviously a mistake to make a closing proposal too early in the negotiating session. Proposing a close before a majority of the issues have been discussed and agreed upon will almost certainly fail. What's more, it will make the remainder of the negotiation more difficult for you, because you will appear overly anxious to close. This appearance may cause your opponent to harden his position or to try to extract more concessions from you as a condition of reaching an agreement.

PART III.

Strategy and Tactics

13.

Winners and losers

In most negotiating situations, the people involved will have to live with each other long after an agreement is reached. Unions must live with management. Sellers must live with their buyers. Employees must live with their bosses. Managers must live with their fellow managers.

When you're dealing with people with whom you have a continuing relationship, it's particularly important not to make them feel that they've "lost" a negotiation. In the short run, people who are dissatisfied with an agreement or who feel that they haven't been dealt with fairly may not live up to their end of the bargain. In the longer run, they may be very difficult to deal with in future negotiations. Revenge, rather than mutual gain, will become their goal.

Oddly enough, it is the way people *perceive* the results of a negotiation rather than the actual results that determines whether someone has "lost" a negotiation. Losers are people who *think* they have lost. When both parties are reasonably satisfied with the results, there are no losers.

In order to come away from a negotiation feeling satisfied, your opponent must feel that he or she has earned each concession and obtained the best deal possible. You should convince your opponent that each concession you make is of real value and is a big concession as far as you are concerned—whether or not it actually is. Don't miss any opportunity to reinforce your opponent's feelings of self-worth. Phrases like "You drive a hard bargain" can be useful for this purpose.

When an agreement has been reached, be careful not to reveal that you think you've gotten the better of the deal. If you feel you have to gloat, wait until you're alone. Don't do it in front of your opponent, if you ever expect to negotiate a similarly successful deal in the future.

In all negotiations, look for ways to help your opponent justify the agreement—to themselves, and to others who are important to them. Make them feel that they got the best possible settlement, and give them ammunition to prove this to others—their boss, their peers, or their spouses.

Don't underestimate the importance of your opponents having a positive feeling at the conclusion of a negotiation. It's the key to your success in other negotiations in the future.

EVERYBODY WINS

Alex Barnes, a young man in Mike Keller's department, had been with the company for a year, and Mike was more than pleased with his progress. He was very productive, and he had shown a great deal of creativity on many of the projects Mike had given him.

Now it was time for Alex's salary review, and Mike was in the office of his boss, George, discussing a raise for Alex. Mike was sure he could get approval for a 5 percent raise, and Alex probably would be satisfied with that. But Mike wanted to do better than that, if he could; he wanted Alex to feel that he had a future in the company.

George, on the other hand, had his own problems. The company hadn't had a very profitable year, and George's budget for employee compensation was pretty tight. He knew how Mike felt about Alex, and if necessary he was prepared to approve a 10 percent raise. He was reluctant to go that high, however, because it would mean that he'd have to give someone else a smaller increase to stay within his budget.

"That's the way it is, Mike," George said. "With things so tight, I don't see how I can approve more than 5 percent for Alex. I know you like him, but I have to think of the whole division."

"The point isn't that I *like* him, George," Mike said. "The point is that he's one of my best people, and he deserves more than an average increase. A 10 percent raise would show him that we appreciate his work and that he has a good future here."

"Five percent isn't a bad increase," George said. "It will keep him ahead of inflation, and maybe we can do better next year when business picks up."

"Well, I'd like to be sure that there *is* a next year for Alex," Mike said. "Five percent isn't *much* ahead of inflation, and I wouldn't want him to get restless and start looking for greener pastures."

"You think that's a danger?" George said.

"I don't know, George. It could be. And it would cost us a heck of a lot more to replace him than it would to give him a decent raise."

"I know, but there's only so much money in the pot," George said. "There are other people who deserve decent raises too."

"And there are others who don't," Mike said. "I'd rather give a good increase to the really productive people and a small increase —or none at all—to marginal performers."

"Yes, but even so . . . . I'll tell you what, Mike. Let's make it 7 percent. Considering our current situation, that's not a bad raise at all. And you can point out that it will also mean that the company will be contributing more money to his life insurance and pension fund, so it's even better that it sounds. Okay?"

"Well—I had hoped we could go a little

higher, but if that's the best you can do . . . .
okay, George, I guess we can live with that."
Mike got up to leave. "I'll tell Alex. And can I
tell him that we expect things to be better
next year?"

"Tell him we'll certainly work for that,"
George said. "After all, we all could use
some more money."

This was a negotiation in which both
parties felt like winners. George didn't have
to go as high as he thought he might, thereby
helping his budget situation. And Mike got
more than he expected, so he was also well
satisfied with the result. It was a collaborative, win-win negotiation in which there were
no losers.

14.

Patience pays off

Nowhere is patience more a virtue than in negotiations. Research has shown that patient negotiators are generally more successful, particularly when they're dealing with impatient opponents.

The best agreements take time to develop; they can't be rushed. Self-discipline and self-restraint can be invaluable assets when negotiations don't seem to be working out or when they seem to drag on and on.

There are a number of reasons why patience plays an important role in successful negotiations.

1. *It facilitates understanding of the big picture.* Patient negotiators are far more likely to appreciate the "big picture" surrounding a negotiation situation. They take the time to try to understand their opponent's goals, to analyze key issues, to evaluate trade-offs and alternatives, and to test their opponent's strengths and weaknesses before committing themselves or their companies to any sort of deal.

2. *It allows opponents to unload.* Very often, nego-tiation opponents will hear very little of what you have to say until they get some things off their chest first. In these situations, no matter how good your arguments, it's best to keep them to yourself until your opponents have had their say. Allowing opponents to talk themselves out or explain their positions fully not only makes them more receptive to what you have to say, but it often results in many issues being resolved without argument.

3. *It gives opponents "digestion" time.* Most people react negatively or defensively when they are asked to accept proposals or points of view without fully under-standing what they're getting into. Even the most legitimate proposal can be flatly rejected if your opponents feel they're being rushed into making a decision. It's wise to give them time to digest or get comfortable with a proposal before asking for a decision. This is expecially true when the proposal is involved or complex. If you push too quickly for decisions, the reaction is likely to be negative.

4. *It allows opponents to tip their hand.* Exercising patience during a negotiation gives you a chance to see how anxious your opponents are to reach an agreement. If they try to rush the negotiations along, it may be a sign that they need the deal more than you do. And the more they try to hurry things along, the more likely they are to make additional concessions.

5. *It lowers opponents' expectations.* Ordinarily, the longer you stick to your initial negotiation position and the more evidence you provide in support of it, the lower will be your opponents' expectations about what they are

likely to accomplish. By patiently holding to your initial position, you send a strong message that you are confident in what you have presented, that your position is serious, and that concessions will be hard to come by.

6. *It provides time to work out a mutually acceptable agreement.* This is probably the most important advantage of patience as a negotiating tool. If both parties to a negotiation exercise patience, it is more likely that the resulting agreement will benefit both sides. This is the essence of true negotiation. Before a negotiation begins, it is difficult to determine how to resolve the problems and issues so that each party benefits. During the negotiating session, additional information is brought to light and new alternatives are discovered, making a mutually beneficial settlement possible.

15.

Active listening

It's obvious that negotiating is a give-and-take process in which, in addition to stating your own case, you have to spend some time listening to what the other person has to say.

The fact is, though, that listening—*really* listening—isn't as easy as it may seem, particularly under the stress of a negotiating situation. People are often so anxious to say what's on their minds that they fail to listen carefully to what their opponents have to say.

Your listening skills can have a direct impact on how well your opponent hears or understands your own arguments. Most people go into a negotiation concentrating on a few major points they want to be sure to make clear. Until they've had a chance to express themselves—to get these ideas on the record and be sure they are understood—they don't listen very well. They're thinking so hard about what they want to say that they don't really hear you. Even though your arguments are well thought-through and convincing, they won't pay attention until they're finished making their pitch.

That's why it often pays to listen first. Let your opponents do most of the talking. Then—when they've got their ideas off their chests and can afford to relax—you can present your arguments. They'll be much more likely to listen to your point of view after they've had a chance to express theirs.

By listening carefully, you can pick up key bits of information that can help you present your case more convincingly. You can often get clues about the needs and concerns of your opponents—what they really want to accomplish. When you know that, you can tailor your arguments and offers to capitalize on this information.

There's another good reason for listening more than you talk during a negotiation: It's difficult for anyone to talk for very long in a negotiation without giving something away. Almost invariably, the person who does the most talking makes the most concessions—or, at the very least, gives away information that is valuable to you.

Improving listening skills

Practicing what might be called "active listening" can increase your chances of success in a negotiation. Fortunately, listening skills can be learned. Here are some ways in which you can develop your own active listening skills.

1. *Minimize the amount of time you spend talking during a negotiation.* It's all but impossible to listen to your opponents if you're doing all the talking. What's more, it's difficult for them to make any concessions,

since you aren't giving them much of a chance. And, as noted before, the more you talk, the more likely you are to give something away—either in terms of material concessions or information about your position.

2. *Show a genuine interest in what your opponent is saying.* This can be done by asking questions about what your opponent is saying and by asking for clarification when you aren't clear on some point. By asking such questions, you are sending a clear message to your opponent that you are, in fact, paying close attention. This strokes your opponent's ego and paves the way for smoother negotiations when it's your turn to talk.

Asking questions also enables you to get additional information about your opponent's real needs and objectives. And it keeps your opponent talking, increasing the possibility that he'll give something away.

3. *Regularly repeat, summarize, and verify what the opponent has said.* This is an important part of active listening, because it helps you to avoid misunderstandings.

On ambiguous points, ask your opponent to spell out exactly what is meant. If there is any doubt about what was said, ask your opponent to repeat the statements. As the negotiation progresses, periodically summarize the results so that it's clear exactly what has been agreed to up to that point. This avoids the danger of proceeding with the negotiation in the belief that some issues have been settled when, in fact, they are still up for grabs.

4. *Clarify the meaning of key terms.* Never assume that you and your opponent have the same under-

standing of exactly what is meant by key terms. Will a late charge be made if the payment envelope is not *postmarked* by a certain date, or if the payment is not *received* by that date? If there is any doubt, nail down the definition of all terms.

5. *Never interrupt your opponent.* Interruptions are discourteous and can put your opponent in a negative frame of mind. In addition, research has shown that people who interrupt often tend to make some kind of direct or indirect concession—perhaps because of their impatience to get things over with.

6. *Take notes during the negotiating session.* Taking notes is important for three reasons: First, it ensures that you are paying close attention to what your opponent is saying. Second, it provides you with a record of what was discussed and what was agreed to. Third, it flatters the ego of your opponent, since people rarely take notes unless they consider what the other person is saying very important. This implicit compliment can put your opponent in a more accommodating frame of mind.

Psychologists tell us that immediately after hearing someone speak, the average person remembers only half of what he has heard. By following these simple guides to active listening, you can greatly increase this percentage. You'll learn more about the people you negotiate with, and you'll enhance your chances of reaching an advantageous agreement.

16.

Limited authority

Negotiators often complain that their negotiating effectiveness is hampered when they don't have full authority to reach an agreement. They object to having limitations placed on how much they can concede to make a deal. They don't like being required to get approval from someone else before they can get a binding agreement.

Purchasing people, for example, often resent the restraints placed on them by company policy, by budgets, or by limitations on the dollar amounts they can spend without the approval of higher management. Salespeople complain that they lose business because of restrictions on their authority to reduce prices, grant discounts, or approve credit sales.

The fact is, however, that having only limited authority in a negotiation can actually *strengthen* your bargaining position. It enables you to cite a boss or an absent principal as the source of your demands or as the reason you really can't make any more concessions. When you don't have any discretion in the matter, a negotiating opponent can't very well expect you to exercise any. You aren't directly subject to your opponent's pressures, because you have no authority to go any further than you have already gone. Nobody can get angry with you if you're offering the best deal you can, given the constraints you're operating under.

Your limited authority will often enable you to get better terms than you would be able to if your opponent knew that you had the power to make concessions or to increase your offer. What can the opponent do if you say something like:

— "I'm sorry, but my boss insists that we get delivery in six weeks."

— "I understand your point, but I have a strict budget, and $15,000 is the absolute maximum I can offer."

— "If it were up to me I might go along with you, but my client won't take a penny under $100,000."

— "My wife would kill me if I paid more than $600."

It's very difficult for negotiating opponents to get around this kind of statement. If they want to make a deal, they'll have to make it within the range that you can approve.

Professional negotiators recognize the bargaining value of having a higher authority to point to as the source of their demands or the reason for their inability to make concessions beyond a certain point. If they don't actually have a boss or a principal they will often *invent* one, just to gain the additional leverage it gives them.

Here are some of the ways in which going into a negotiation with limited authority can give you a bargaining advantage:

- *Having authority limits lets you say "no" tactfully.* You aren't being unreasonable; you simply don't have the authority to do what your opponent wants you to do. Being able to say "no" without antagonizing your opponent can be valuable, particularly when you want to maintain a friendly, long-term working relationship with your opponent. You can say, "I think your proposal has merit, but my boss won't buy it in its present form." This shifts the blame from you and enables you to disagree without harming your personal relationship with your opponent.

- *Your authority limits can permit your opponent to back down without losing face.* It's difficult for a negotiator to make a concession without receiving anything in return. But if you can say, "I'm sorry, Frank, but $3,000 is all I have in my budget, and the boss won't give me a cent more," Frank may decide to take your offer, even if it's at the low end of his acceptance range. And he won't feel unhappy about it; after all, he got all there was to get!

- *Authority limits can enable you to get additional time to evaluate a proposal.* During a negotiating session, you'd sometimes like to give more thought to the ramifications of a proposal your opponent has made. It's always a mistake to let yourself be rushed into an agreement when you don't fully understand all its implications. In these situations, it's useful to be able to cite your limited authority to get the extra time you need to evaluate a proposal: "It sounds good to me, but I'll have to check with my boss before we make it official." This not only buys you some think-time, but it makes it legitimate for you to reopen negotiations on parts of the proposed agreement that you decide are not advantageous. You aren't repudiating an agreement; you're merely relaying your boss's objections.

• *Your limited authority may give your opponent an added incentive to deal directly with you.* There are times when you're close to reaching an agreement but your opponent is still pushing for something that you don't want to give up. If you point out that you don't have authority to make such a concession, your opponent may have second thoughts about pressing the matter. Rather than risk having your boss reopen issues that you have already agreed on, or perhaps even losing the deal altogether, your opponent may decide that a bird in the hand is worth two in the bush. It may be wiser to settle for an agreement within your authority limits, rather than taking a chance on what might happen if another party is brought into the negotiation.

Using agents

Because of the advantages of having limited authority, you can often negotiate better for someone else than you can for yourself. And the converse is also true: Often someone else—an agent—can negotiate better for you than you could for yourself.

Agents aren't principals. They can resist the pressures from opponents during negotiations because they can always fall back on their limited authority: "My client won't let me agree to that." When you have an agent negotiating for you, the agent can work out the best deal he can get, then come back to you for approval. Since you haven't been a party to the negotiations, you aren't obliged to accept the terms that have been negotiated. You are perfectly free to reject anything you don't like and send your agent back to negotiate further.

The agent-principal relationship needn't be a formalized one. In buying a house, for example, many husbands and wives have found it useful to act as "agents" for each other. The husband may visit the house, and after being shown around, express interest. "But," he tells the owner, "my wife definitely wants a modern kitchen. If we were to buy this house, we'd have to spend four or five thousand dollars to modernize the kitchen, so you'd have to reduce your asking price." If he gets agreement, he goes home to "talk it over" with his wife. Later, she visits the house. "It's lovely," she tells the owner, "but my husband says it would cost a fortune to carpet it. If we buy the house, will you leave the wall-to-wall carpeting?" In this way, they gain valuable concessions before any actual negotiating has taken place.

When you do have someone else negotiate for you, don't give your agent unlimited authority to reach an agreement. If you just say, "Get the best price you can," your agent has no way of knowing what your goal or your minimum expectation is. And when an agreement is reached, you'll have the nagging feeling that the agent might have done better with some more effort.

Before the negotiation determine with your agent a goal that you both consider attainable. The agent must believe that the goal is realistic in order to be committed to reaching it. What you're saying, in effect, is, "Here is the objective we've agreed on. If you can get it, that's fine. If not, come on back and we'll talk about it some more."

When opponents lack authority

There are times, of course, when the shoe will be on the other foot, and you will find yourself negotiating with an opponent who doesn't have full authority to reach a final agreement. Early in the negotiation, you should find out exactly how much authority your negotiation opponent has. If the opponent doesn't have full authority, any concessions that you give up during the course of the negotiation may be viewed as final and binding—while your opponent's concessions are subject to the approval of a higher authority.

Some negotiators purposely send a subordinate into a negotiation with very little authority. This representative's job is to extract all the meaningful concessions he can, while keeping his concessions subject to higher-level approval. When you have reached what seems to be a final agreement, the representative submits it to his boss for approval. The boss accepts the concessions you have given up, then reopens negotiations on the points he does not approve.

No matter how fair and reasonable you have been in dealing with the subordinate, and no matter how much you have already given up, the person with full authority will almost always press you for further concessions.

There are several ways to deal with this kind of situation.

- *Refuse to negotiate with someone who does not have full authority.* Whenever possible, avoid negotiating with people who don't have the authority to reach a final agreement. Find out early in the negotiation whether your opponent can negotiate a binding agreement. If the answer is no, insist on negotiating with someone who can.

When this is not possible, you might consider having someone else act as *your* agent in the negotiation—or you might "invent" a higher authority for yourself, so the agreements you reach will have to be approved by your boss as well.

- *Make concessions grudgingly.* When you must negotiate with someone with limited authority, be stingy with your concessions. Don't give up too much negotiating room. Remember that your opponent's boss is going to want to open up negotiations again and will expect you to give up even more.

- *Nail down the agreement one piece at a time.* A good way to deal with opponents with limited authority is to insist that each time an issue is agreed on they go to their boss immediately and get the agreement on the issue approved. This accomplishes two things: First, it protects you from having the boss come in at the last minute to reopen negotiations on the final agreement, since the boss has already ratified it—one piece at a time. Second, having to obtain approval on each issue can wear down your opponent, since it can be a tedious process. The opponent may reach the point of insisting that the boss deal with you directly—which is what you wanted in the first place!

17.

Linking issues

Linking issues during a negotiation can often get you better results than you could achieve by treating them separately. Linking simply means tying an agreement on one issue to an agreement on one or more other issues.

For example, suppose you want to sell a fairly old camping trailer and a fairly new pickup truck. If you sell the two pieces separately, chances are that the truck will sell fairly quickly, but you'll be stuck with the run-down trailer. But if you link the sale of the two pieces of equipment into a package deal in which you won't sell one without the other, you'll probably be able to get a fair price for the package.

Advantages of linking

There are a number of situations in which linking can improve your performance during negotiations and help you get a better deal.

1. *Linking can help you overcome areas of negotiating weakness.* Successful negotiators often link an issue on

which they are weak to an issue on which they're strong. For example, assume that a purchasing agent is trying to negotiate a new contract with a supplier, and the seller has tried to strengthen his bargaining position by bringing up the fact that the purchasing agent's company was slow in paying the seller's invoices during the past year. To offset this, the purchasing agent might reply, "Since you're bringing up the issue of my company's slow payment, let's also discuss why your company has had such poor delivery performance and why there were so many back orders." By linking these issues, the purchasing agent has moved his negotiation position from one of relative weakness to one of parity, and quite possibly to one of relative strength.

2. *Linking can force the opposition to deal with certain issues on your terms.* This approach was used by a man who was being interviewed for a mid-level management position. He had an impressive track record, and the company made him an attractive job offer that he was anxious to accept. He knew, however, that his success with the new company would be determined, at least in part, by the operating budget he was given to get the job done.

Rather than accepting the offer outright, he linked his acceptance of the job to the company's acceptance of his operating budget. Management looked over his proposed budget and agreed that it was reasonable. If he had tried to negotiate the budget *after* he accepted the job offer, his negotiating leverage would have been greatly diminished, and the result might not have been nearly as favorable.

3. *Linking can force concessions from your opponent.*
Another way of using the linking strategy is to tie one
issue to another and then claim that your opponent's
position on the issues, as a package, is not acceptable. For
example, a purchasing agent could say to a seller, "I can
live with your payment terms, but not at that price." If
the seller wants the deal badly enough, he'll concede on
the payment terms or the price. If the seller holds firm on
both issues, but still shows signs of wanting an agreement, the purchasing agent could then link a third issue
to the other two to try to gain a concession. He might say,
for example, "At that price and under those payment
terms, I have to have better service and faster delivery
before I can agree to any sort of deal."

Linking issues together in this manner is usually quite
successful, because it provides a negotiation opponent
with an opportunity to concede something and still feel
good about the deal.

Pros and cons of linking

Linking issues gives you a good opportunity to make
trade-offs, one issue against the other. It also puts
pressure on your opponents to reach agreements on all
the issues, because each issue is linked to others, and
failure to settle one issue can jeopardize the whole deal.
Linking can sometimes be the only way to get action on
issues that the other party doesn't want to deal with.

On the other hand, linking can also work against you
in some circumstances. It can give your opponent an
opportunity to use a minor disagreement on one issue as a

means to try to force you to make concessions on another issue. If the issues aren't linked, but are dealt with separately, an opponent can't prevent agreement on one issue by objecting to another.

You have to decide which approach—separating issues or linking them—will be most advantageous to you. Linking issues gives you more room to make trade-offs, but if you feel strongly about individual issues, you will want to deal with them separately.

18.

Gambits and ploys

There are a great number of negotiating tactics that experienced negotiators resort to in an attempt to gain an advantage over their opponents. Once you've been taken in by one of these ploys, you're likely to recognize it the next time someone tries it on you, and you'll be on your guard. In this chapter, we'll describe some of the more common tactics so you'll be able to recognize them and protect yourself against them. A tactic that is identified as a tactic loses its effectiveness. Not only are you not fooled by it, but being "caught in the act" will often embarrass your opponents and put them at a disadvantage.

In the chapter on "Negotiation Ethics" we discussed some unethical tactics that you may occasionally run into. The tactics in this chapter are usually not unethical, but they can be costly to you if you don't recognize them and deal with them.

Emotional outbursts

Emotional outbursts are often used as a negotiation tactic—even at the highest levels. Most of us remember or have read of the time when Nikita Khrushchev, the Russian leader, beat on the table with his shoe at a meeting of the United Nations.

This display of emotion was not exactly spontaneous; some observers say it wasn't even his shoe, but one supplied for the purpose. The same thing is true of most emotional outbursts by negotiators: They are planned, timed, and staged to assist your opponent in gaining an advantage. You should treat all displays of emotion during negotiations with suspicion and disbelief.

The first step in handling emotional outbursts is to recognize that they are merely tactics designed to persuade you to provide concessions without getting anything in return. Relax, remain calm, and show your opponent that you are not affected by playacting.

When the outburst subsides, toss the monkey right back on your opponent's back. Ask for an exact and specific explanation of what the fuss is about. What is it in your proposal that your opponent doesn't like? Demand specifics, not generalities. If there is something wrong with your proposal, your opponent can point it out and you can deal with it. If your opponent is bluffing, that will be apparent because there will be no specifics to point out.

If you deal with emotional behavior calmly and rationally, you can nullify its effect, and your opponents will think twice before trying such tactics on you in the future.

Verbal bullying

A similar tactic, most often used in group sessions, is verbal bullying. One participant, usually a man, raises his voice, pounds the table, and tries to intimidate you while you're expressing your views. Sometimes this can be handled by waiting until the outburst is over, then thanking the bully for his clear and forceful expression of his opinion. If this doesn't quiet the bully, remain calm and continue to make your point. You can even lower your voice to emphasize the contrast between your mature demeanor and his childish behavior. Eventually, his conduct will become an embarrassment to everyone, and your case, presented with calm assurance, will appear stronger.

Making threats

In commercial transactions, the implied threat that one party or the other will break off negotiations is always present. It's acknowledged that either party has the option of taking his business elsewhere if a satisfactory agreement is not reached.

Outright threats are less common, but they do occur. They are a poor negotiating tactic, because a threat often provokes a counterthreat, anger and hostility are aroused, and the chances of conducting productive negotiations are greatly diminished.

If you are threatened during a negotiation, your response will be determined by the answers to two questions: How credible is the threat? If the threat were carried out, how much would it hurt me?

The credibility of a threat depends on whether the other party has the ability and the willingness to carry it out. If an opponent threatens to destroy your business if you don't make a minor concession, you may well doubt that he could do it—or you may doubt that he would take such drastic action over a minor point. For this reason, large threats are often less credible than small ones.

If you believe an opponent could and would carry out a threat, you must assess how much damage would be done. If you could live with the results, a strong response is to imply that the threat really doesn't concern you. Your opponent must then wonder whether you are bluffing, and reconsider what it would cost him to implement the threat.

When possible, particularly when the threat is subtle or merely hinted at, it's often best to ignore it, as if you didn't hear it or didn't understand it, and continue to negotiate. An opponent who isn't sure of what your reaction means—whether you didn't understand the threat or are simply not bothered by it—will be off balance, and may decide that continuing to negotiate would be more productive than trying to intimidate you.

The best time to deal with threats is before they occur. The more dependent you are on the person you're negotiating with, the more vulnerable you are to any threats. A negotiating opponent who is your only supplier or your only customer, for example, is in a position to do much more harm to you than one who is only one of a number of customers or suppliers. Make it a point to develop alternatives that will lessen your dependence on any one source, so the costs of a serious disagreement will be reduced.

One of the most intimidating tactics is the threat of invoking the law. Few people relish the idea of becoming involved in costly and time-consuming litigation. Many bargaining issues involve legal questions that an opponent can claim will be resolved against you. Some negotiators will concede a point rather that take a chance on being brought into court.

If legal questions are likely to come up in a negotiation, have legal counsel available at the end of a telephone to respond to them. If you expect that legal problems will be involved in the negotiation, have an attorney with you at the session. You will be at a disadvantage if your opponent is represented by legal counsel and you are not.

Bait-and-hook proposals

Some proposals are designed to seem complete until you accept them. Then you find that you've accepted a proposal with a number of strings attached, and you're put in the difficult position of backtracking.

In one case, the manager of a parts distributorship asked the union business agent for a proposal when the collective bargaining contract was nearing expiration. In a few days, the business agent called during lunch hour and left a message: "We'll settle for an 8 percent wage increase for each of the next three years."

The manager was delighted; the increase was well within his budget. He didn't know much about negotiating a union contract, but he thought he should jump on the offer before the business agent changed his mind. He fired off a letter accepting the offer. A few days later, the business agent came to his office with the letter in hand and said, "Fine. I'm glad we're agreed on wages.

Now, in addition, we also want another week of vacation, dental insurance, an increase in the pension program...."

The manager was the victim of an incomplete proposal, and it took the help of the company labor counsel to reverse the damage. The moral is clear: Never accept a proposal until you're sure it is complete and that you fully understand it.

Lowball proposals

The purpose of the lowball proposal is to offer a low initial price to attract the buyer, then make up the difference by adding on accessories, cost overruns, special charges, and other additions later. Many types of industrial equipment are offered in this way, as are automobiles, cameras, and even government contracts.

Before you agree to any proposal, be sure that everything you expect to receive is spelled out in writing. Then negotiate every extra added to the base, and call for cost justifications for the value of each item. This may be time-consuming, but it yields the best results.

The sucker punch

Sometimes negotiators want some information they're afraid their opponent might not be willing to supply if asked for it directly. So they use an indirect approach similar to a sucker punch in boxing.

An experienced boxer will sometimes leave an opening so inviting that the opponent cannot resist throwing a punch. In doing so, however, the opponent leaves himself open to a counterattack. In negotiations, the sucker-punch approach takes the form of a statement that is so annoying that the opponent will rush to correct it. This reaction reveals exactly what the other negotiator wanted to know. For example:

"Your increase in productivity must have been over 10 percent last year."

"Ten percent? Our increase was only 6 percent."

Unlike the boxer, who finds out immediately that he's made the wrong move, the sucker-punch recipient in this kind of exchange may not realize for some time that he's become his own worst information leak.

Here are a few ways to avoid giving away information that you'd rather keep to yourself:

1. Don't answer questions too quickly. Always pause long enough to analyze why an opponent is asking a question.

2. Watch for statements designed to irritate you. They are often attempts to induce you to say things you wouldn't otherwise say.

3. When you catch an opponent trying to draw you in, simply identify the statements or questions as guesses. After being caught a few times, an opponent is less likely to try to use this tactic.

The moral appeal

Opponents who are having difficulty justifying their positions with facts and logic often resort to "moral" arguments. If they get anywhere with them, they'll use them again and again.

When you're accused of taking an unfair position, being avaricious, dealing unkindly, being inconsiderate, or anything of that nature, don't retract and don't retreat. If an opponent says, "That's unfair," simply replying, "It seems perfectly fair to me" may be enough to quash the protest. If not, ask your opponent to explain the reasons for his or her position and take a good look at them.

The concept of fairness is so difficult to define that the use of the term in negotiations is almost meaningless. What seems fair to one person may seem quite unfair to another. A person who tells you, "I can't make any money at that price" may have a different idea of what constitutes a reasonable profit than you do. Before you make any concessions on the basis of such an appeal, demand verification and check the facts.

Attempts to arouse your sympathy are another form of "moral" appeal. When your opponent frowns, shakes his head in despair, winces, or otherwise appears distressed, don't let your sympathy run wild and offer additional concessions. That's exactly what your opponent is trying to get you to do.

Appeals to fairness are usually attempts to get you to evaluate the situation through your opponent's eyes, on the apparent assumption that the opponent's criteria for judgment are better than yours. They shouldn't influence your position unless they can be substantiated by proof.

This is not to say that morality shouldn't be a serious consideration. But as they are employed in negotiations, "moral" arguments are usually a ploy used by the side that has the fewest facts and the weakest logic to support its demands.

19.

Telephone negotiations

Negotiating with someone on the telephone can be dangerous. There are many things that can go wrong. It's easier to misunderstand someone over the phone than in face-to-face talks. Often, you don't have enough time to think, and important things can be omitted. If the other person has called you, you're likely to be unprepared and disorganized. And it's easier for the other person to say no than it is in a face-to-face situation.

Nevertheless, telephone negotiations can be useful under certain conditions, as long as you're careful to keep control of the situation. Here are some cases in which telephone negotiations can be advantageous.

1. *When the dollar value involved is small.* Time is money, and it obviously isn't economical to spend a day (including travel time, lunch, and meeting time) to negotiate an agreement that at best will save you a negligible amount of money.

2. *When the issues are few in number.* The less complex the negotiations, the less the need for face-to-face contact to resolve the issues.

3. *When the parties are a considerable physical distance apart.* Your potential gains from a negotiation may not be great enough to justify the time and expense involved in traveling to negotiating sessions.

4. *When a great deal of preliminary detail is involved.* Much of the detail work—such as clarifying proposals, disposing of minor issues, and obtaining pertinent information—can be handled more efficiently and economically by telephone.

On the other hand, you shouldn't attempt to negotiate by telephone when large amounts of money are involved, or when the negotiations involve complex and important issues. And never let a telephone call pressure you into negotiating when you aren't thoroughly prepared.

Negotiating by telephone

Negotiations by telephone can be successful, if you conduct them under favorable circumstances. Here are some guides to keep in mind.

1. *Be fully prepared.* When you're going to make a call to negotiate with someone, or when you're expecting such a call, prepare yourself before the call, just as you would for a face-to-face negotiation. If you're called by someone you aren't prepared to talk to, listen, get the full story, then call back later.

2. *Get needed materials together.* Have everything you need at hand before the call—files and paperwork on the subject, a calculator, paper, and whatever else you will be using.

3. *Make an agenda.* As with any negotiation, you should prepare a list of the topics to be discussed and check them off as you go along. This will insure that you don't miss any points and that your opponent doesn't use the absence of face-to-face contact to dodge any issues.

4. *Take notes.* Make a written record of everything that is discussed; don't trust to memory. Confirm agreements in your own words to insure that both parties understand what has been agreed upon.

5. *Be prepared to hang up.* If things aren't going well in the negotiation, have a good excuse ready to hang up and rethink your strategy. Breaking off a negotiating session is almost always easier over the phone than in face-to-face negotiations.

Part IV.

Team Negotiations

20.

Negotiating as a team

Most of the negotiating done by managers who aren't professional negotiators is informal and conducted on a one-to-one basis. There may be times, however, when you are asked to be part of a negotiating *team*—perhaps because of your expertise on a subject or your familiarity with a certain area.

The principles and strategies we have been discussing in this book apply equally to team negotiations. But negotiating as a team is more complicated. Chances are, each team member will have a different set of perceptions and perspectives. This is not entirely undesirable, since the purpose of a team is to harmonize contrasting viewpoints.

Your opponents, however, may try to take advantage of the situation by using a "divide and conquer" strategy to exploit the differences of opinion among your members.

How can you overcome this problem? The first step is to get your team to agree on a common set of goals before you start. But no matter how carefully you plan, things will come up during the negotiations that you haven't taken into consideration. So the real key is to agree on agreeing.

A united front

One way to display a united front is to delegate all the speaking authority to one chief negotiator. Although this tends to reduce the usefulness of the other members of the team, it may be necessary if they are inexperienced negotiators.

Another approach is to agree on areas of expertise and refer relevant questions to the designated expert on the subject. All engineering questions, for example, would be referred to the chief engineer, and the other members would support his or her statement, whether or not they agreed with it.

If there is disagreement among members of your team, save the arguing for the caucus room. If you think another member of the team is out of line, take the earliest casual opportunity to call a caucus meeting to resolve the difference. (Don't call a caucus the instant a disagreement occurs, or you will alert your opponents to the fact that there is disagreement in your ranks.)

The lowest common denominator

When team members disagree at the negotiating table, the opponents will work toward the lowest common denominator—that is, they will take the side of the member whose position is closest to their own. They will also look for other "cracks in the plaster" by trying to pit members against each other. In doing this, they hope to be able to discover and support the members whose views are most favorable to them.

Open disagreements also make future negotiations more difficult. Expecting the same kind of indecisiveness and disorganization at the next session, your opponents will raise their sights and shoot for higher objectives.

Disagreeing outside the negotiating room can be worse than disagreeing inside. After adjourning for the day, someone from the other team may try to get one of your members off to the side to get his impressions of the meeting. If a disgruntled team member takes this opportunity to sound off, the impact can be worse than a disagreement during the negotiating session.

When you are negotiating as a team, disagreements among your members will almost always result in losses to your side. To keep this from happening:

1. Make sure your negotiating team agrees on a common set of goals.

2. Devise a common strategy to accomplish these goals.

3. Make sure all members agree on agreeing, at least publicly.

4. Save all disagreements for the caucus room.

21.

Practice makes perfect

Many managers seem to think that if they're thoroughly familiar with the facts in an area to be discussed, they're ready to negotiate. Actually, there's a lot more to it than that.

You may be a good golfer, but if you're facing an important match and you haven't played in a couple of months, you'd certainly want to play some practice rounds first. And if the match was to take place on a course you'd never played, you'd try to shoot a few practice rounds on that course to familiarize yourself with its characteristics.

Negotiating is quite similar. Most of us are involved in important negotiations rather infrequently—perhaps only two or three times a year. It takes a little time to get our negotiating game in shape. And negotiating on new topics or with new people is like playing a new golf course: You aren't sure of the distances or the slope of the greens, and you don't know exactly where the hazards are.

Laying the groundwork

Before the negotiation begins, particularly if the issues are important, you should allow adequate time for preparation and practice. The first step is to study the situation to determine what alternatives are available and which are the best from your point of view. Without this kind of forethought, you may enter negotiations without a clear idea of exactly what you're trying to achieve. That's a good way to lose before you start.

When you've established your objectives, you need time to put together the best possible case. Professional negotiators often spend twice as much time preparing as they do negotiating.

Finally, it pays to allow some time to rehearse your act. Hold a practice session in which one of your colleagues represents the opposition. This kind of practice can help you have the best questions—and the best answers— available for the actual negotiating session.

The role of role playing

Role playing—conducting mock negotiating sessions before the actual negotiations—is an excellent way to practice. Inexperienced negotiators tend to write off role playing as silly or a waste of time; experienced negotiators recognize its value in sharpening their negotiating skills.

The role-playing process is equally well suited to practicing one-on-one negotiations and team negotiations. When you're going to conduct the negotiation yourself, you can act out the negotiation with a colleague.

Circumstances permitting, you should take the time to play both roles. This will help you gain insight into both sides of key issues.

Once the role-playing session begins, it won't take long before you realize that your game needs a little tuning up before you enter the actual negotiating session. With your colleague playing a devil's advocate role, you'll soon discover which of your negotiating skills are in need of improvement. After the session, you can concentrate on overcoming these weaknesses. You may want to conduct more role-playing sessions, depending on the importance of the negotiation, before you feel ready and confident.

The role-playing process is similar when the negotiation involves a team. In this case, of course, you'll need a group of colleagues to play the role of the opposing negotiating team.

How role playing helps

Role playing provides a number of important benefits:

1. Since neither the individual nor the firm suffers any permanent consequences as a result of the role-playing sessions, individuals or teams are free to try out different approaches and tactics without fear of failure or reprisal. This allows you to try your negotiation strategy and get the bugs out of it before putting it into action.

2. Role playing draws attention to important facts and issues that may have been overlooked during the planning phase. These issues may not come into focus until the role-playing session is well under way. It's far better to discover them during a trial run than to be surprised by them during the actual negotiating session.

3. Playing the role of the opposition allows you to put yourself in the other person's shoes. Research has shown that negotiators often do a poor job of assessing their opponents' goals before a negotiation. Yet expert negotiators will tell you that negotiation success is much more likely if you are thoroughly familiar with your opponents' position and what they want to accoomplish.

4. While dealing with a role-playing opponent, you have an opportunity to develop well-organized arguments to counter proposals or responses that your real opponents may come up with.

5. For negotiating teams, role playing provides an opportunity for group members to get to know each other and learn to function as a team, rather than as a group of individuals. Because each person brings his or her own ideas and biases to the group, it may take more role-playing sessions to prepare the team than would be needed for an individual.

Worth the effort

Role playing is nothing new. It has been used in many fields to gain a competitive edge over an opponent. Football teams, for example, sometimes practice by having some of their men play the parts of key players of their next opponent. Lawyers often have colleagues play the roles of key witnesses while they examine and cross-examine them. They may also play the roles of witnesses while their colleagues examine them. They have found this exercise useful for revealing areas in which they were not well prepared and for providing additional insight into key witnesses.

In preparing for a negotiation, role playing can mean the difference between success and failure. The experience of successful negotiators has shown time and again that it's well worth the effort to role-play a negotiation situation before the actual negotiation begins.

22.

The home court advantage

In sports, most teams tend to win more games on their home court or home field than they do when they're on the road. The home court advantage can be very important.

That's also true in negotiating. Studies of negotiations conducted at home and away indicate that you're more likely to be successful in negotiations that take place on your home turf. The home team has a number of advantages.

- *Greater physical comfort.* Serious negotiations can be extremely hard work, in terms of both physical and emotional demands. Being well rested and mentally alert can be important factors in the success of negotiations. When you conduct a negotiation on your home turf, you sleep in your own bed the night before and eat familiar food before sitting down at the negotiating table. As a result, you're more likely to begin negotiations feeling well rested and ready to go.

A number of factors can prevent visiting negotiators from feeling their best when they arrive at the negotiating table. After a tiring trip they may be tense and have difficulty falling asleep. Hotel beds may be uncomfortable, the halls and adjacent rooms noisy, the heating or cooling system uncooperative, and the wake-up service unreliable. All this can leave them less than bright-eyed and bushy-tailed negotiators the next morning.

• *Increased control.* When you're negotiating in your home court, you have much more control over the situation. You have a fairly free hand to arrange the physical setting of the negotiations—the size of the room, the shape of the table, the kind of chairs to be used, and the availability of chalkboards, projectors, and other equipment. You can be sure that you have everything you need to present a convincing case.

• *Resource availability.* Home-court negotiators usually have access to more resources than do their visiting opponents. If records or files are needed to substantiate an argument or prove a point, they can be made available almost immediately. If the testimony of expert witnesses or technical specialists such as engineers or quality-control personnel is required to move the negotiation along, these people are available. And if high-level approval is needed to resolve unanticipated problems or issues, this can be quickly arranged.

• *Psychological advantages.* As host, you are in a position to show certain courtesies to your visitors which they, being human, will feel a desire to acknowledge some way in return. This can create an agreeable atmosphere in which the negotiations are likely to run smoothly.

When you negotiate at home, your opponents are

coming to you. This gives you a subtle psychological edge, since it implies that the visitors have a stronger need to reach an agreement. This factor can be seen in international negotiations: When, for example, a Middle Eastern country wants arms, its representatives come to the United States. When the United States wants to negotiate an oil agreement, our representatives go to the Middle East.

There's no place like home—usually

This doesn't mean that you should adopt a hard-and-fast policy of refusing to negotiate anywhere but at home. For one thing, it won't always be possible. And there are circumstances in which you will be better off negotiating away from home—for example, when it is desirable to verify, firsthand, claims made by negotiating opponents, or when it might be necessary for your opponents to get higher-level approval to resolve certain problems or issues.

On the whole, however, the advantages that go with your home territory make it the preferred place to negotiate whenever possible.

23.

Put it in writing

Most things that are worth negotiating are worth putting in writing. It's best to write while you negotiate, setting down the main points of agreement as you go along. Then you can get this rough agreement initialed at the negotiating session, rather than waiting until the next day.

Putting the points of agreement in writing can help you avoid problems like these:

• With nothing in writing, it's hard to be sure that the parties have not misinterpreted each other. When disagreements later come to light, they may delay the signing of a final agreement.

• It's difficult to remember all the details that were agreed to if the writing is put off until a later time. Pieces are more likely to be left out, leading to misunderstandings and disagreements.

• If the other side wants to back out of an agreement, it's easier for them to fabricate a misunderstanding when nothing has been put in writing.

If you can't get the whole agreement put in writing at the time of the negotiation, at least try to get an outline of the main points. Even though additional wording will have to be added later, getting the outline agreed upon at the meeting will minimize future problems.

The negotiation log

In a court of law, a written transcript is made of everything that is said during an entire trial. This makes it possible for anyone to go back and review the testimony.

A complete transcript of this kind is expensive. A simpler system is to keep track of what is said during negotiations in the form of a negotiation log.

Here are the major points that a negotiation log should include:

1. *Preliminary discussions.* Any definitions, clarifications, etc. should be noted.

2. *The opening offer.* Note the initial offer and the terms and conditions included in it.

3. *Counteroffer.* The same information should be noted for the initial counterproposal.

4. *All changes to the initial offers.* Each new proposal should be recorded, as well as each proposal that is accepted.

5. *Descriptions and modifications.* When evidence to support a position is introduced, a notation should be made indicating its impact on the negotiations.

6. *Concluding agreement.* Before leaving the table, both parties should review and initial the terms and conditions of the agreement that has been reached.

24.

Keeping negotiation records

You shouldn't have to start from scratch every time you prepare to negotiate with people you've negotiated with in the past. If you've kept careful records of previous sessions, you'll have a head start for the next time.

Memory is a notoriously unreliable thing. You can't expect to remember all the details of a negotiating session that was held months or even years ago. Besides, negotiating teams change, and some members who will be participating in the new negotiation may not have taken part in earlier sessions. That's why successful negotiators categorize and file any information that might be useful in the future.

Information to keep

Here are some of the kinds of information that can be extremely valuable and should be kept on file.

1. *Cost information.* Solid cost data are not easy to come by. You can't expect your opponents to furnish you with a complete breakdown of all their costs at the beginning of a negotiation session. But facts about cost

structures are sure to come out during negotiations. By keeping track of these bits of information, you'll gradually be able to put the puzzle together.

2. *Previous negotiation logs.* Smart negotiators take notes at every session to make sure they don't miss any vital information. A negotiation log outlining all the offers and counter offers that led to an agreement should be kept on file. It will prove useful for assessing the future concession behavior and reactions of your opponents.

3. *Personal information.* For each company you do business with, you should keep a file of information on the individual negotiators. This file should include the names of *informal* leaders; background information on individual negotiators, such as education, other jobs held, and personal hobbies or outside interests; and notes on subjects or approaches that should be avoided with certain individuals.

Keeping records of this kind may be a chore, but some day they may be worth their weight in gold.

Resistance to record-keeping

If records are so valuable, why do negotiators sometimes neglect to maintain them? There are several reasons. For one thing, they are sometimes sure that, given the intensity and mental concentration of the negotiations, they will remember all that is really necessary. But no one can expect to remember everything that would be recorded in notes taken as the negotiation goes along. Even negotiators with good memories may fail to take into consideration the value of the information they have in their heads to other people who may some day take their places.

Keeping records and creating files takes time. When time is at a premium, the record-keeping function may be put off until later. During the session itself, it's often necessary to concentrate on the thoughts of the moment rather than to write down what is happening. When the negotiations are over, it is tempting to relax and rest rather than to fiddle with records. And when other business must be attended to, it is easy to forget to get back to the completion of the records. Moreover, negotiators are evaluated on the basis of the outcome of the negotiations, not on the records they set aside for the future, so record-keeping seems like an unnecessary frill to some negotiators.

Record-keeping can be tedious. It's not the exciting part of the negotiations. In fact, many people who are considered good negotiators are really good only at the "talking" part of the process. That's why well-organized teams put the record-keeping responsibility in the hands of one designated individual who may have no other function in the negotiations.

Sometimes the notes may be so disorganized that even the negotiators have difficulty making sense of them a few weeks later. Someone else may find it impossible to unscramble a tangled collection of notes. So negotiators sometimes feel that it's pointless to keep notes that no one will be able to understand anyway.

Some negotiators are reluctant to create a file of this kind for fear that it will fall into the wrong hands; some people who have access to the file may indiscriminately talk about its contents. So some negotiators destroy their notes at the end of the negotiations to prevent them from being misused.

A little care is needed

None of these problems is insurmountable. With a little care, the essential security of the file can be arranged, and the file can be organized in a way that makes it useful in the future. The time required will be well spent, and the contents of the file will often prove invaluable in other negotiations.

25.

Conducting a debriefing

As millions of Americans watch on television, the astronauts guide the space shuttle to a safe landing and disembark. After days in space and the tension of the landing itself, they are undoubtedly tired. Nevertheless, they are immediately hustled off to a debriefing session.

Why the rush? Because the sooner a debriefing session is held, the better. In the case of negotiations, the negotiating team can immediately reflect on what took place during the negotiating session. They can recall the events and the words that seemed to make the deciding differences. They can analyze what went right over the course of the negotiations as well as why some things went wrong. The debriefing session is where planning begins for future negotiations.

Negotiators are often reluctant to go into a debriefing session immediately after finishing a long negotiation. They will come up with a variety of arguments for putting off the debriefing or eliminating it altogether:

Argument #1. "We're tired. We'll be able to think more clearly tomorrow (or next week)." Wrong. Studies have proved that you will remember more immediately after the negotiating session than you will later, even if you are very tired.

Argument #2. "I've got a good memory. I'll remember everything tomorrow just as well as I will today." Not true. Psychological studies have proved that almost everyone forgets a significant portion of an experience within a few hours after it happens.

Argument #3. "We'll probably never have to deal with these people again, so there's no point in rehashing the results." Perhaps. But most negotiators find a debriefing of great value as a learning aid. Negotiators who fail to debrief lose an excellent opportunity for self-improvement.

Argument #4. "We already have a written record of the session. What more do we need?" Lots more. The debriefing is designed to *analyze* the event that took place—not just to recite a blow-by-blow historical record.

Debriefing gives the negotiating team a final opportunity to get together. It allows the team leader to assess the need for additional training for less-experienced members, and it aids in the selection of future negotiating teams. It also allows the team members to pat themselves on the back and prepares them psychologically for future negotiations.

Using a checklist

The negotiation is over. You've got the team together,

and you're ready to debrief. Where do you start? What points do you cover?

It's a temptation just to start analyzing whatever sticks in your mind. Usually, though, you'll find that too many important points are missed by such a free-form discussion. A debriefing checklist is useful to be sure that you analyze these key points:

1. *Was the basic goal properly established?* Well-planned negotiations always have a goal. In the light of the experience of the negotiation itself, was your goal justified, or did you over- or underestimate what you could win?

2. *Was the basic goal revised during the negotiations?* If it was, what caused the revision, and was it justified? Many negotiators, looking back, can see that they were tricked into lowering their expectations by the opposing team—or even worse, by their own misreading of the situation.

3. *How close did we come to meeting or exceeding our basic goal or our revised goal?* This step is simply a comparison of the results of the negotiation with your expectations.

4. *What was the opponent's apparent basic goal?* This is a much harder question to answer; it will usually involve a certain amount of guesswork. But from what you learned when preparing for the negotiation, and from the opposing team's behavior during the nego-iating sessions, you should be able to make a pretty good judgment.

5. *How satisfied was the opponent with the outcome?*

Your negotiating opponents probably didn't get everything they wanted, but they may still be satisfied if they think they got the best deal possible. This is desirable if you expect to be doing business with them in the future. If they feel that they were squeezed to the point where they will lose money, prestige, part of their market, or something else that's necessary to their long-run survival, they are probably dissatisfied. Unhappy opponents may have little incentive to hold up their end of the agreement and may refuse to negotiate at all on future deals. (Incidentally, don't be fooled by disappointed faces on the other team: good negotiators don't want to appear to gloat when they think they've come out ahead.)

6. *What things went right?* Look at the various strategies and tactics that you employed and assess those that seemed to work best.

7. *What things went wrong?* Analyze possible mistakes. Did you fall for any of your opponents' tactics? Did any of you do or say something you shouldn't have? Did any of your tactics backfire?

8. *Where did the major breaks come?* Look back over the negotiations and try to assess what factors, strategies, or tactics led the way to the final accord. What were the turning points?

9. *Was preparation adequate?* It's important to determine what information you could have used, but did not have with you at the negotiating table.

10. *How did the team work together?* What can you do to improve your teamwork?

Every negotiation situation is different, and it may be necessary to include additional factors in your checklist to adapt it to your particular situation.